THE GHOSTLY TALES OF SALEM

Published by Arcadia Children's Books
A Division of Arcadia Publishing
Charleston, SC
www.arcadiapublishing.com

First published 2024
Manufactured in the United States

Designed by Jessica Nevins
Images used courtesy of Shutterstock.com; p. 2 Wangkun Jia/Shutterstock.com; p. 8 Paul Brady Photography/Shutterstock.com; pp. 12-13 Jaclyn Vernace/Shutterstock.com; pp. 20-21 AlessandroV/Shutterstock.com; p. 36 Dee Browning/Shutterstock.com; p. 104 Dominionart/Shutterstock.com.

ISBN: 978-1-4671-9778-6
Library of Congress Control Number: 2024939049

Spooky America

The Ghostly Tales of Salem

BETH HESTER

Adapted from Ghosts of Salem: Haunts of the Witch City by Sam Baltrusis

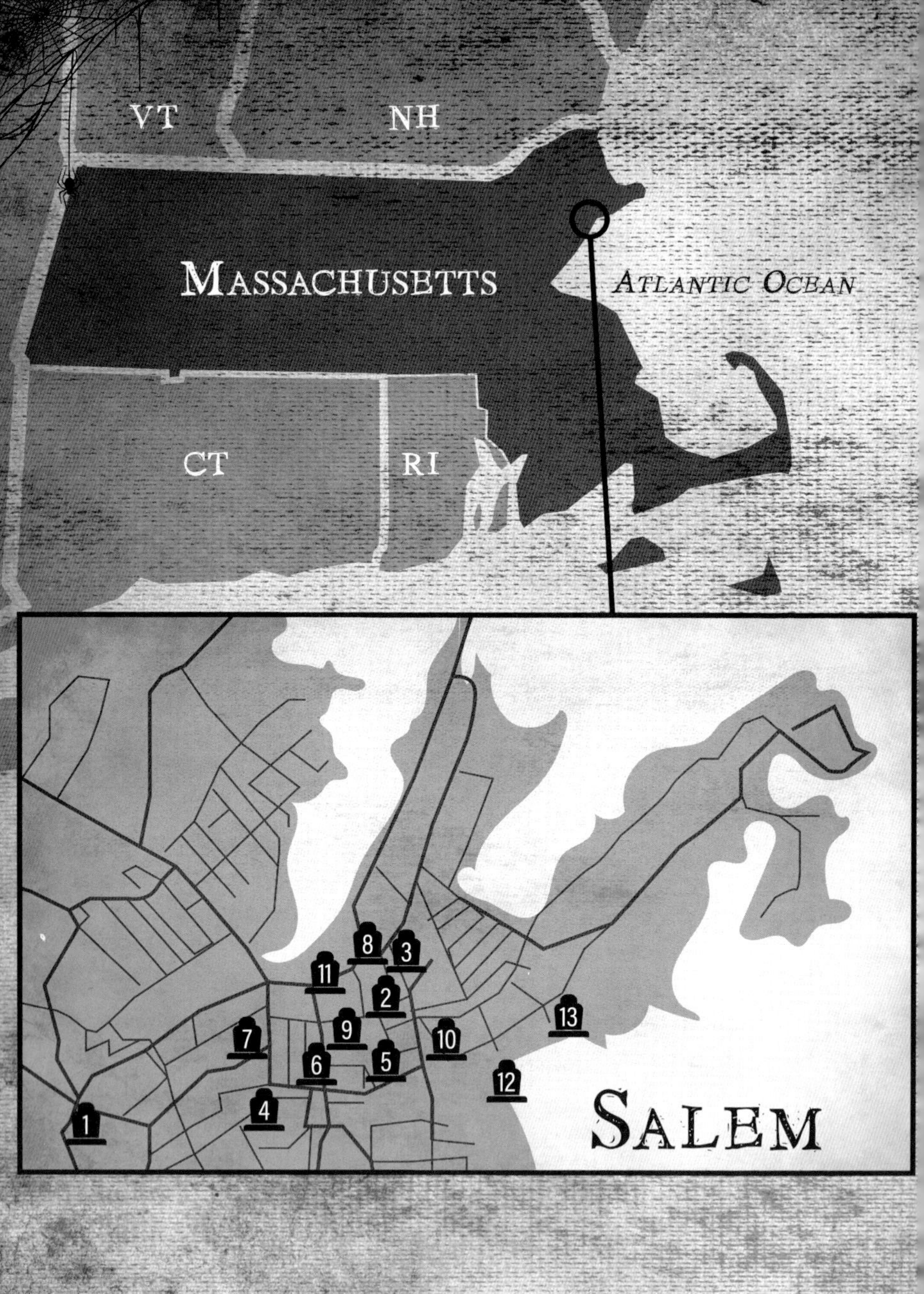
VT
NH
MASSACHUSETTS
ATLANTIC OCEAN
CT
RI
1
2
3
4
5
6
7
8
9
10
11
12
13
SALEM

Table of Contents & Map Key

Salem Maritime National Historic Site

Welcome to Spooky Salem!

If you're familiar with this coastal New England town, you know how much there is to explore here. Salem is one of America's oldest towns, offering a glimpse into the Puritan past. It's a maritime hub—a historic port with cool old ships along a storied waterfront. It's a creative place where people come to get inspired by the art of the beautiful Peabody-Essex Museum and the legacy of Nathaniel Hawthorne, nineteeth-century author of classics such as *The Scarlet Letter*. There's one more thing about Salem that you've probably heard, even if you're unfamiliar with this little city north of Boston. Its nickname might ring a bell: Salem is sometimes called "Witch City."

Many locals have mixed feelings about this moniker. Salem's "witchy" identity mostly plays out in lighthearted fun and sold-out hotels during Haunted Happenings ("the largest celebration of Halloween in the world," according to the official event website). Every October, restaurants are fully booked and souvenir shops make a bundle selling T-shirts, bumper stickers, and miniature broomsticks to tourists. People dress up, tour groups fill up, and everyone seems to have a great time. (Well, everyone not actively looking for a parking space.) But locals know that the words "witch" and "Salem" (derived from the Hebrew word for "peace") have a very dark history, too. Salemites don't always like to dig into that side of the past . . . but sometimes the ghosts just won't let it go.

As New England author and historian Sam Baltrusis writes, "Salem somehow manages to embrace its dark, witch-trials past while simultaneously shutting a door on it." In his book *Ghosts of Salem,* Baltrusis opened the door on some of this city's darkest stories to show where the ghosts, spirits, poltergeists—and yes, maybe even witches—are hiding in the not-so-peaceful shadows.

We've gathered the most gripping ghost stories and haunted hotspots in this book. Do you dare to peer into the darkness? Come along—it's time to explore spooky Salem!

Salem, Massachusetts

SALEM WITCH MUSEUM

Gallows Hill

What is Gallows Hill? Here's how Salem author Nathaniel Hawthorne described it: "This was the field where superstition won her darkest triumph; the high place where our fathers set up their shame, to the mournful gaze of generations far remote. The dust of martyrs was beneath our feet. We stood on Gallows Hill." Gallows Hill is where the victims of Salem's 1692 witch trials were unjustly put to death—executed by hanging and buried in a shallow ditch.

This place is named for the "gallows," a structure from which a condemned person is hanged to death. When it comes to Salem's Gallows Hill, it's as straightforward as that: it is where the hangings took place. (Historians

now think trees were used in place of actual gallows.) Then again, it's also much, much more complicated than that.

THE WITCH TRIALS

In 1692, hundreds of men and women in Salem were charged as suspected witches. The idea itself wasn't unique to Salem—charges of witchcraft happened in other cities and in other countries, too. But the intensity of Salem's trials—the many accusations, the fervor of the prosecutors and jurists, and the way suspicion and fear took hold of the community—would earn these infamous proceedings a dark place in history.

It started with rumors and vague accusations. For example, a "witness" might have a vision in which a neighbor signed "the devil's book." This could lead to a trial, a conviction, and even an execution. The

The Salem Witch Trials Memorial

stakes were life and death, but for those accused of witchcraft, building a defense was near impossible. Guilt and innocence weren't determined with solid evidence. A dream might be enough to convict someone. Suspicion, paranoia, and panic ruled the day inside and outside of the courtroom.

How did Salem's witch trials get so out of hand? Good question. It takes a lot of people making a lot of bad decisions—or not nearly enough people standing up in defense of fairness—to let so much harm take hold. If the town named for peace had been truly at peace before the trials began, it may have been better prepared to defend itself. Alas, Salem wasn't peaceful in the times leading up to the witch trials.

The Stage Is Set

In early 1692, Salemites were recovering from a difficult winter and devastating outbreak of smallpox, a deadly disease that spread quickly and had no cure at the time. Aside from hunger, cold, and sickness, there was a constant threat of attack from outside the town. Inside, there was a growing feeling of distrust as shifting fortunes left families eyeing their neighbors with jealousy. Puritans in the colony, who had expected Salem to be a haven for their religion, eyed non-Puritan newcomers with nervousness. England, which still ruled over the Massachusetts Bay Colony, had just overthrown its king. The culture and political shape of the colony was changing. The governor was new. It seemed nothing at all was certain. People were anxious, scared . . . and eager to cast blame.

The Cases Begin

Two young girls, ages nine and eleven, were the first among "the afflicted girls" —so called because they suffered fits of uncontrollable twitching and convulsing. The girls said it was because they'd been bewitched by an enslaved woman, Tituba. Then they blamed others, too. Even though society at the time paid little attention to young girls, claims such as this could set the courts in motion . . . and that's exactly what happened. Along with a handful of other girls, these two were the source of most accusations during the witch trials.

A new court had to be set up to conduct the many trials. In the new court of "Oyer and Terminer" ("hear and decide"), the panel of judges could find someone guilty based on "evidence" we wouldn't even recognize today. Take "spectral evidence." According to this theory, a witch could appear in someone else's vision or dream. The catch? Only a witch could accomplish this, only the accuser could observe it, and there was absolutely no way to defend against it. A guilty verdict typically meant one thing: death on Gallows Hill. Justice was swift and harsh . . . and it didn't look much like justice at all.

By the time the hysteria settled down, hundreds of suspected witches, including men, women, and children, had been tried in court, and twenty people had been killed.

Gallows Hill Today

Where is Gallows Hill? Nathaniel Hawthorne certainly found it hard to forget. As strange as it might seem, however, there were many years when people weren't really sure of the exact location. Then, in 2017, new research at last led to an official announcement: the place where nineteen innocent men and women were wrongly hanged for witchcraft was identified as Proctor's Ledge. A memorial was put in place, giving Hawthorne's "generations far remote" a place to cast a "mournful gaze," honor the lives lost, and think about that strange moment in history.

The official memorial might be new, but some tour guides and historians were finding their way to this wooded place behind Walgreens long before the announcement. In *Ghosts of Salem*, Sam Baltrusis identifies clues that lead here, including court notes of 1692 testimony from Rebecca Eames, who described seeing the gallows from Boston Street on her way to downtown Salem.

Former ghost tour guide Mollie Stewart's experience on the site is recounted in Leslie Rule's *When the Ghost Screams*: "As Mollie ventured up the hill, she at first didn't think too much of it when she heard voices. She figured it was just a few other people, out exploring. But then she spotted a hooded figure. As she stared, it vanished before her eyes."

At Witch House (the former home of Judge Corwin, who presided over the trials), a guide once had a surprising conversation with a Gallows Hill spirit and recorded it on an electronic voice phenomenon (EVP) recorder. The guide described the incident this way: "We came to the base

Home of Judge Jonathan Corwin

of the hill. One of the questions we asked was 'Are you a condemned witch?' and we picked up a distinct 'no.' We got out of there as quick as we could!"

People think the current-day Gallows Hill Park may be the location of the shallow ditch where bodies were left after the executions. This certainly seems like a sure-fire recipe for a haunting: an unjust execution and an improper burial. Maybe that's why full-bodied apparitions have been reported there. People report seeing strange balls of light and hearing

phantom voices. Records show that a few of the bodies of the executed were retrieved by family members shortly after their deaths so they could be buried with proper respect in their family plots. It's unclear what happened to the others. They might have been retrieved by a kind neighbor or a nearby church. It's also possible they were left behind by the frightened Salemites of 1692. If so, they may wander here still, shining as orbs of light . . . calling out to Mollie . . . waiting to see who might come to visit them next.

St. Peter's Church

Philip & Mary English

Not everyone accused of witchcraft wound up on Gallows Hill. Some were declared not guilty of their alleged crimes. Others, like Philip and Mary English, escaped.

The Perfect Targets

Philip English was everything Salemites loved to hate. He was new to town, a rich merchant with a fleet of twenty-one ships. He built a grand house for a new age, while his neighbors, tied to the old economy, were struggling. His native language was French, not English. His religion was Anglican, not Puritan. And he always spoke his mind. When longtime Salem residents tried to push him around to show they were in charge, Philip English pushed right back. If all that wasn't enough, he was said to be reluctant to pay taxes, but "overfond of litigation." In other words, he really liked suing people he thought owed him money. So, when people were being arrested for witchcraft in the spring of 1692, attention soon turned to the high-profile merchant who always seemed to be rubbing neighbors the wrong way.

On April 18, Philip's wife, Mary, was arrested on suspicion of witchcraft and imprisoned on the second floor of the Cat and Wheel tavern. Philip visited her three times a day . . . until a warrant was issued for his arrest one week later. Thanks to the couple's political connections (and friendship with Governor Phips, the colony's new leader), they were able to move to a jail in Boston with very lenient terms. They could leave during the day and return at night, basically like lodgers in a hotel. However, they still faced the terrible prospect of a trial in Salem. It was hard to imagine that would go well! So, with the help of a preacher, the couple managed to escape to New York.

While they were in New York, Philip and Mary followed the news from Salem. In the summer, they learned that there was a shortage of food due to a drought, so they sent a ship filled with food to help. Then, when the frenzy of the trials was over, and Governor Phips issued a general pardon, the Englishes went home.

Back in Salem

When Philip and Mary returned home, they were distraught to find that Sheriff George Corwin, the same man who had arrested them, had helped himself to whatever he wanted from their mansion. Philip was determined to recover his lost valuables from Corwin—or at least to sue the corrupt lawman for the $2,000 or so worth of stolen furnishings. Philip also held a furious grudge against one of the witch trials' leaders, Judge Hathorne, whom he blamed for all his family's troubles. He also blamed Puritan Reverend Noyes, whom he called a murderer. Yet the greatest heartache was soon to come: one year after they returned to Salem, Mary English died during childbirth.

Philip would live another forty-two years without his beloved Mary. He spent the rest of his life getting into trouble over taxes and suing people to try to recover his lost property. But he never did get back the value of his confiscated property. And there was yet another blow: two of his granddaughters would marry grandsons of the judge he despised, John Hathorne.

Before he died, however, Philip made a gift to Salem that would leave a lasting mark in more ways than one. He donated his land in downtown Salem to be the site of a new Anglican church.

Here to Stay

The first Anglican church in Salem, St. Peter's was a wooden structure built in 1733. It featured a small cemetery, eventually with twenty-three graves, including Philip English's final resting place (one of only three known burial sites of accused witches in America).

In 1833, St. Peter's would be rebuilt in granite, with the new structure covering part of the cemetery. Some parts of the original building were carried over into the new building, including the pews from the 1733 structure and an original wooden door. The grave markers would be moved more than once for their own protection (and so they wouldn't be buried under the chapel addition). But the skeletal remains they marked would stay buried in place. Maybe that's why people see ghostly apparitions hovering around the burial site. Could these ghosts be looking for their mismatched markers?

Today, the headstones are arranged in two small plots on either side of the church's front door. In the same area, witnesses have

spotted ghostly figures against the graveyard's back wall, seeming to watch people walk by on the sidewalk. People also report seeing a female figure emerging from the salvaged 1733 door. According to Sam Baltrusis, "A female spirit, wearing shackles, is reported to appear emerging from the eighteenth-century structure. Some believe the female figure is Mary English."

Perhaps the most interesting apparition at St. Peter's Church is the one said to belong to Philip English—even though everyone seems to agree that he has updated his look for the times! If you walk by St. Peters, look for a "modern-looking guy" with a bald head. He'll be the one crouched behind a gravestone, peering out. You might also spot him inside the church, if you're lucky. If you haven't caught a glimpse of him by the time you leave, however, don't lose heart: some people check their photos later and find out he's right there in the pictures they took after all, even though the photographer is *certain* there was nobody there before. . . .

If you still don't see Philip English, there is one more place to try. Head over to the Remember Salem gift shop next time you're in the neighborhood, and *he* just might *see* you. He might have a message for you, too. One former employee recalls hearing a male voice calling clearly over the shop's loudspeaker, "I see you. I watch you." If Salem is ever tempted to overlook the lessons of the past, that speaker just might click on again with a friendly (or not-so-friendly) reminder from the outspoken

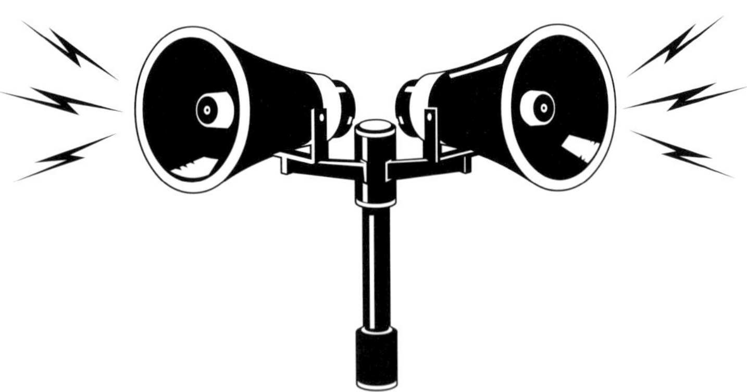

English, a French-speaking Anglican merchant who knows how to hold a grudge. If you're shopping for souvenirs and hear a strange voice call, "I see you. I watch you," it might be Philip English warning you to watch your step around his stuff. (But beware: if you hear him say "I sue you," you might want to get a good lawyer. . . .)

Charter Street Cemetery

Cemeteries

The graveyards at St. Peter's Church are thought to represent twenty-three Salemites from times past, but they aren't the oldest cemeteries in Salem—or the most haunted. The following are three storied cemeteries that have been offering a home to Salem's dead—and running shivers up the spines of the living—for centuries.

Howard Street Cemetery

Twenty people were killed during the witch trials hysteria, with nineteen of them executed on Gallows Hill . . . so where was the other one? Right here. In 1692, where Howard Street Cemetery sits now, the cruel Sheriff George Corwin stood over elderly landowner Giles Corey and demanded Corey surrender and confess to witchcraft. When Corey refused, Corwin piled rocks on top of the suspect's chest.

"Do you confess?" the sheriff demanded.

Corey did not. Corwin called for his men to add more rocks on top of Corey.

"Do you confess?"

The ordeal continued into a second day, with Corey steadfastly refusing to confess in the face of torture, and Corwin unfazed by the old man's suffering as his men added more and more rocks to the pile. After two days, on the brink of death, Corey muttered a curse: "Damn you, Sheriff. I curse you and Salem!" And with that, Giles Corey died . . . crushed to death by Sheriff Corwin.

With a history like that, it's not surprising that this is considered Salem's most haunted cemetery. Adjacent to Old Salem Jail and the keeper's house, this place has been surrounded by high drama from the start. Considering Giles Corey's terrible end, there's an eerie coincidence about the people buried here. It's said that around fifteen percent of them died by being crushed to death. Benjamin Ropes was killed on the ship *Belisarius* when the mast collapsed and crushed him. Ten people died in the jail when a floor gave way.

Others buried here echo Corey's story, too. The Essex County sheriff's offices once overlooked the graveyard. Through the years, many of the staff have died of heart attacks or other heart-related ailments. That includes the infamous Sheriff George Corwin, who died of a heart attack just a few years after killing Corey.

Even people who visit the cemetery today report feeling a heaviness in their chest, as though their bodies are sympathizing with Corey's pain.

Other hauntings unseen by the naked eye become clearer in photographs: people take photos of an empty graveyard, only to discover creepy details later, such as groups of shadowy faces or ghostly flames in the background. Tim Maguire of Salem Night Tours reports:

"Someone on my tour took a photo of the cemetery. By the end of the tour that person came forward to share the photo they took. Definitely not what we were looking at. There seem to be figures of people standing over someone. Most people feel like they found the spirit of Giles Corey or have seen his apparition. They think it's a reminder of what we have done to him there."

When it comes to seeing Corey's ghost in person, most people in Salem would rather not. They take his curse seriously. After centuries of observation, Salemites think they understand the rules: If the ghost of Giles Corey appears to you, Salem burns. If the ghost speaks to you . . . you die.

Nathaniel Hawthorne

seemed to agree with the warning about fire when he wrote that the apparition "of the wizard appears as a precursor to some great calamity impending over the community." In 1914, the town perhaps had its proof. Over the course of a few days, the sheriff's department received almost 300 reports that an old man in tattered clothes was hanging around Howard Street Cemetery. Many of those who spotted him said they had tried to offer him help, but he had vanished before they reached him. Sheriff deputies went to Howard Street Cemetery to check it out, but they found only an empty

cemetery. Nevertheless, they stayed there to monitor the scene. They watched the location for hours. Nothing happened, so the deputies left. About half an hour later, the flames took hold. The Great Fire of 1914 would devastate Salem, burning about two-thirds of the town. Giles Corey may be gone, but his curse lives on in Salem.

Broad Street Cemetery

On a quiet night in Salem, you might hear an otherworldly whistling sound weave through Broad Street Cemetery and see orbs of light float by as though dancing to the crooked tune.

Older than Howard Street Cemetery (but still not Salem's oldest), Broad Street Cemetery is a pretty spot for an evening walk near the Salem Inn and the Witch House. It doesn't get quite as much attention as some other haunted hotspots (something its most famous residents might be very happy to hear). In fact, you might be the only person there when you visit. Well, the only *living* person.

Broad Street Cemetery is the final resting place of two of the most notorious villains of the Salem witch trials: Judge Jonathan Corwin

and Sheriff George Corwin. They're quiet company now, but that wasn't always the case. In the panicked spring and summer of 1692, most people in Salem were terrified of George Corwin. In October, however, the feeling of hysteria that had gripped Salem began to break (largely because the accusers went a step too far when they accused the governor's wife of witchcraft). Governor Phips had issued a general pardon and disbanded the court, which put an end to the proceedings and transformed George Corwin from all-powerful prosecutor into Salem's most hated villain.

Suddenly, the panic that had clouded people's judgment seemed to clear. At last, Salemites were able to see that Sheriff Corwin was a cruel, horrible person. Did they also understand their own fault? Maybe they did, or maybe that would take a little more time. But people seemed to understand that the sheriff who was supposed to protect them had abused his office and led them very badly astray . . . and they were furious.

Corwin lived only a few more years, despised and shunned by the community. He died of a heart attack in 1696, at just thirty years old. That left the Corwin family with a problem: if they buried him in a town cemetery, they thought the people of Salem might be mad enough to dig him up and take revenge. Instead, they buried him in the basement of their own house first, waiting a few years for tempers to cool before moving his remains to Broad Street Cemetery. (His uncle, Jonathan, would join him there later.)

People who visit Broad Street Cemetery sometimes wonder if the ghostly whistle sound they hear might have anything to do with Jonathan or George Corwin. However, both ghosts seem to be attached to other locations:

Jonathan Corwin is said to haunt the Witch House (his residence during life). George Corwin's spirit is said to haunt the place where his body was first buried, now the site of the Joshua Ward House.

So, who is the mysterious whistler? First, here's an eyewitness report from the October 1975 *Boston Globe*: "All of a sudden, a glimmer of white caught my eyes . . . .There, on a grave to the right, was a man's shoulder, the shadow of his head was turning, and out from his mouth came a jagged, whistling sound."

The apparition, who wears old-fashioned clothes and sometimes appears confused, is thought to be the lingering spirit of Jonathan Neal. Neal was a carpenter from Marblehead and the grandson of one of the area's earliest settlers. He reportedly died in a freak accident while walking alone one night in 1790. Whistling drunkenly on his way home from a "house of intemperance" (that, is, a pub), Neal tripped and landed head-first in the mud to meet his sticky end. It was one year after the U.S. Constitution was signed—the start of a new nation—and the end of old Jonathan Neal, feet-up in the boggy field. With all those Corwins in the neighborhood, we're glad he joined the crowd. It's nice to have a bit of music in the place.

Charter Street Cemetery

Known also as "Old Burying Point," this first Salem cemetery was built before 1637. It's likely the oldest colonial-era cemetery in the United States. Sitting adjacent to the Witch Trials Memorial, it's also the grand finale of many witch and ghost tours of Salem—so you're not likely to find it as peaceful as Broad Street Cemetery, for instance. One thing it does have in common with Broad Street, though, is a witch trials villain: Judge John Hathorne.

Hathorne was one of the presiding judges in the special court of Oyer and Terminer in 1692. Like his friend Judge Corwin, he ignored the counsel of other esteemed judges to strike the use of so-called "spectral evidence" and to reconsider the methods used in the trials. Judge Hathorne's great-great-grandson, Nathaniel Hawthorne, would write of his ancestor, "... [he] made himself so conspicuous in the martyrdom of witches, that their blood may

fairly be said to have left a stain on him." Judge Hathorne himself didn't seem to mind: he never apologized for his role in the witch trials, living in Salem another twenty-five years in relative peace after they were over.

Nathaniel Hawthorne, on the other hand, was appalled by his family's involvement in the witch trials hysteria, even changing the spelling of his name to distance himself from the judge. Yet something brought Nathaniel Hawthorne back to this cemetery again and again. It wasn't visits to the family tomb, though. His sweetheart, Sophia Peabody, lived in a house immediately next door, so the young Nathaniel came here often while courting her. Sophia, who suffered from headaches, preferred to take walks at nighttime.

Hawthorne—already disposed to a melancholy and romantic imagination—happily agreed, and the two enjoyed many late-night walks through the cemetery as they fell in love. This place didn't just inspire their romance. As they walked, Hawthorne also eagerly read the old-fashioned names on the grave markers and adopted some of them for the characters in his books.

Nathaniel and Sophia aside, many people report a feeling of heavy sadness when they walk through the cemetery grounds. Is it the closeness of the Witch Trials Memorial that makes the air feel so melancholy? Or perhaps visitors are sensing a pair of ghosts, sometimes spotted near the back of the graveyard: a mother and son. It's thought their story might be related to a tragic fire that took place at an inn on Charter Street long ago. The boy's father stayed behind to fight the flames and was killed in the blaze. Did these two spirits return after death to try to find him?

Another business next to the cemetery, Murphy's Restaurant, once had a surprise visit from one of the cemetery's residents once. Local lore says that a casket once broke through a wall and fell right into the building!

The "lady in white," however, is a Charter Street spirit who seems less interested in jump-scares . . . and more motivated by love. Seen often as orbs of light, occasionally as a figure in photographs, she is thought to be tied to a particular gravestone that reads, "Mary Corry." People believe this is an alternate spelling of "Mary Corey"—the second wife of Giles Corey, who was crushed to death by Sheriff George Corwin. Mary was said to be Giles's great love in the 1600s. In the many years since then, her ghostly apparition has been witnessed in the cemetery as well as nearby parking lots and buildings. Sam Baltrusis suggests:

"The lady in white has been seen coming from the general vicinity of her grave marker, and many believe it's her spirit that continues to levitate across the cemetery headed toward the Howard Street Cemetery in the area where her beloved husband was pressed to death . . . . Perhaps Mary's spirit is searching for her tortured husband . . . and if the two spirits finally meet, the curse will be undone."

Haunted Houses

Are ghosts making things go bump in the night at these spine-tingling structures? We can't be sure . . . but you might have some theories after you hear their haunted histories!

Gardner-Pingree House

It was 1830, and Joe Knapp was worried. Until recently, he'd expected his mother-in-law, Mrs. Beckford, to inherit a large amount of money . . . money that would eventually come to Joe and his wife. He figured Mrs. Beckford would get about half of Captain Joseph White's $200,000 fortune, as long as White didn't write a will saying otherwise. So far, there was no will, and Captain White was eighty-two years old—practically ancient for those days! Knapp figured the old man would die any day, and the fortune would be as good as his.

So, why was Joe Knapp so worried? To his horror, he had just learned that Captain White had recently written a will after all. The captain had just finished writing the document, as a matter of fact . . . and it didn't leave Mrs. Beckford nearly the fortune Joe Knapp had been planning on. Joe did NOT want to give up that money. If only the new document didn't exist, he thought. If only the old man had died before anyone knew about it. Hmmm. The sinister wheels turned in Joe's mind. If only there were a way he could make those things true . . . .

Joe and his brother Frank hatched a plan. They had only to make the document disappear . . . and of course make sure the captain died before anyone knew it was missing. Then Joe could live happily ever after with his $100,000.

THE PLAN:

Part 1: Joe steals the will.

Part 2: The brothers hire a skilled assassin. The assassin makes a clean kill, leaving no trace of evidence.

Part 3: White is found dead. A mystery!

Part 4: Police investigate and assume a robbery gone wrong.

Part 5: The Knapp brothers win!

WHAT ACTUALLY HAPPENS:

Part 1: Joe steals what he *thinks* is the will (but isn't).

Part 2: The brothers hire assassin Richard Crowninshield. Crowninshield stabs the captain thirteen times, hits him over the head with a custom-carved hickory-stick club, and drops the club on his way out of town.

Part 3: White is found dead. The hickory-stick club is recovered. Richard Crowninshield is overheard talking to his brother about the crime.

Part 4: Police investigate and quickly rule out a robbery, since nothing is missing. The Knapp brothers suggest robbers are on the loose and quickly come under suspicion. Crowninshield is arrested. The Knapp brothers are arrested. Crowninshield dies in Old

Salem Jail. U.S. Senator Daniel Webster—one of the top lawyers in the country—is hired to lead the prosecution against the Knapp brothers.

Part 5: Knapp brothers win? Nope. Daniel Webster wins—he got a $1,000 fee and gave a closing statement described as "the greatest argument ever addressed to a jury." Stephen White wins. He was the relative who actually inherited the fortune, as directed by the new will (which had been filed in a local law office the whole time). But Joe and Frank Knapp? No, they most definitely lost.

The two brothers were hanged in front of Old Salem Jail later that year, about three months apart. Their story continued to captivate, however. Authors Nathaniel Hawthorne and Edgar Allen Poe both found inspiration for their own stories in what Webster called a "cool, calculating, moneymaking murder."

The house where it all happened still bears ghostly traces of the dramatic story. Visitors claim to have spotted signs of Mrs. Beckford in the house or felt a strong female energy as they walk through the space. Others walking along the sidewalk outside the house just might see old Captain White, looking right back out at them if they happen to glance up toward the second-story window (the window where Joe Knapp would have loosened the bars so his murderous accomplice could gain access).

Photographic evidence is strong, according to Tim Maguire of Salem Night Tours. He says he often surprises skeptics on his tours by bringing them to the Gardner-Pingree House. They arrive convinced they are about to debunk stories of hauntings . . . and wind up with their own bit of Salem lore to bring back home.

Joshua Ward House

The house is named for Joshua Ward . . . but the hauntings that earn it a spot in this spooky collection are connected to a different character you might remember from previous stories: Sheriff George Corwin—the short-tempered sheriff known for arresting and torturing people during the 1692 witch trials. Corwin's own house once stood on this very site.

In the years after the hysteria of 1692, people in Salem despised Sheriff Corwin and his cruelty. To recap from the story on page 38, when he died of a heart attack just a few years later, in 1696, his family was too afraid to bury him in a town cemetery. They were sure the furious people of Salem would dig up his body or desecrate his grave. So instead, his family buried him in the basement of his own house. When things calmed down a few years later, Corwin was reburied at Broad Street Cemetery. He remains there today . . . well, physically, at least. Some think his spirit may want to stay close to his first gravesite, where the Joshua Ward House now stands.

Over the years, visitors to the building have reported objects being turned over, papers scattered on the floor, and candles being bent into shapes. Corwin's ghost has been spotted in one room. More frequently, however, people have seen or sensed a female presence who has become known as "the lady in black." Could this be one of Corwin's victims seeking revenge? His victims would probably feel pretty angry, maybe even vengeful, after being treated with the kind of violence the sheriff was known for. Consider these accounts of the lady in black: She seems to prefer women, who sometimes are able to see her. It's men who feel her attacks. Sometimes her targets felt scratches on their chests. Others reported a terrifying tightening around their throats, as if they were being strangled.

In 2015, the Joshua Ward House at 148 Washington Street was transformed into a hotel called "The Merchant," celebrating Salem's rich maritime past. The ghosts may have finally found some peace. There have been no new reports of hauntings in the fancy new hotel.

Ropes Mansion

Judge Nathaniel Ropes was forty-eight years old in 1774, and he didn't see any reason why he should change his politics now. He was a Tory, just like always: a loyal servant to the king. Sure, sometimes his guests liked to argue about politics and try to get him to change his mind. Five years before, John Adams had come for lunch, and the two men had sat in the front hall for ages talking politics, with Adams going on and on about how the judge should change sides and become a patriot, or whatever nonsense. A passing fad, surely. But the judge had been gracious enough, hadn't he?

But talking with Mr. Adams in the front hall was one thing. Now this mob of rowdies was throwing things at his house, demanding his allegiance. It sounded like clumps of dirt and big gloppy mud balls and—was that a rock? Good heavens.

The revolutionaries were indeed throwing mud and stones at the judge's home. America was on the brink of revolution against Great Britain and its monarch. Judge Ropes had always shown loyalty to the crown, so his neighbors wanted to know: Are you with us or against us? They demanded he come out and give his answer.

On this day, however, Judge Ropes wouldn't be answering that question . . . or any question. As the patriots shouted their demands, the judge lay in his bed upstairs, suffering from smallpox. He would die the same day, a Tory to the end.

Centuries later, the building's caretakers, Rick and Georgette Stafford, had taken new photos of the house for an insurance appraisal. As they sat down to review the pictures, they were amazed by what they saw in one particular shot of the front hallway. Hovering just over the couch was what looked like a pair of ghostly hands—just where a man's hands would be if he were sitting on the couch beside a friend, arguing politics after lunch. Was this Judge Ropes, possibly reconsidering his position after all this time? Maybe forty-eight wasn't too old to change your mind. Maybe 248 wasn't too old, either. It just goes to show: there's always time to reconsider.

The second Ropes family ghost in the house is the judge's relative, Abigail "Nabby" Ropes, who died seventy years later. Nabby was tending a fireplace when her clothing caught fire—a terrifying accident that left her with burns that would cost her her life.

These days, Nabby can occasionally be seen peering out of a second-floor window or even standing in the house as a full-bodied apparition, her long, dark hair twisted back in a bun. According to the *Salem Gazette*, Nabby's cause of death was "a distressing illness of three weeks caused by her clothes accidentally taking fire." Another article from the 1980s allowed for a more sinister view: that perhaps others in the house *chose* not to save her: "Abigail's servants never heard the screams for help, or so they said."

Does Nabby blame those servants for her death? Perhaps that's why her spirit still lingers in the house, where people think her ghost could be responsible for fallen dishes, screams late in the night, odd taps on the shoulder, and, of course, unexplainable fires.

Old Salem Jail

Between 1813 and 1991, people sentenced to jail time in Salem would find themselves locked up at Essex County Correction Institute (aka "Old Salem Jail") right next to the Howard Street Cemetery and the site of Giles Corey's gory death. (Just in case things weren't scary enough in jail!) In other towns, judges could send each convicted person to the prison that suited them best: a juvenile detention center for young people on a first offense, for instance, or a maximum-security men's prison for notorious serial killers. But not in Salem. Here everyone was together in the same building: men on one side, women on the other side, and children in between. (Children? That's right. There are stories of inmates as young as four years old serving time for breaking household items, in the same building that would hold the Boston Strangler and hitman Joseph "the Animal" Barboza.)

In the 1860s, Confederate soldiers captured during the Civil War may have been packed into the jail, too. By the 1880s, the building was so crowded that an extension had to be built to fit all the inmates. Some say the addition, with its two striking cupolas (small rooftop towers), was built using rocks salvaged from nearby St. Peter Street. The legend is that the rocks may have been cursed—stained with the blood of the witch trials. No modern plumbing was installed with the addition.

Cursed or otherwise, a decade later, Salem Jail was back in its usual desperate condition: overcrowded and putrid. By that time, around fifty people had been executed by hanging (including the Knapp brothers in the 1830s, for arranging the murder of Captain White, the story told starting on page 55).

Inside the cold stone walls, the grim conditions endured for decades. By the 1970s, people "doing time" in Old Salem Jail still used chamber pots instead of toilets. (There were two toilets for the whole facility, so each prisoner got a turn to use one once a week.) There were fights and murders. Everyone—inmates and guards alike—complained of the stink and the roaches. Finally, in 1991, the jail closed. "We won," wrote an inmate in toothpaste on the wall, thrilled to be moving to another jail—*any* other jail—rather than Old Salem. Some shadowy cellmates, however, seemed reluctant to leave.

The building that was once Old Salem Jail is now a block of luxury apartments. Before that, however, it stood vacant for a number of years. Would it surprise you to know that teenagers snuck in to look around during that time? They probably hoped to find some cool souvenirs like a prison meal tray or one of those old chamber pots (*ew*). Instead, they brought out stories of eerie inmates still lurking around the old prison. Some people heard whispers and metallic sounds echoing through the empty structure. Others spotted a residual haunting—a scene that replays like a video, without reacting to the world around it. They saw a figure (perhaps a prisoner from long ago?) holding a candle while walking across the floor from room to room . . . only the "floor" was long gone—it had fallen through years ago!

Other apparitions inside the former jail include those tormented soldiers from the Civil War, whose ghostly figures complain of the captors' harsh punishments. With their pained groans and old-fashioned uniforms, the soldiers became so familiar over the years, that 1980s prisoners learned to just shrug and introduce them as "residents."

Not everyone wants to stick around forever, though. Outside the building on the prison

grounds, you just might see a quick-moving shape out of the corner of your eye, a shadow figure darting across the yard, or even a full-body apparition racing toward the chain-link fence. It could be one of those Old Salem Jail ghosts trying to make a break for it after all.

Restaurants & Bars

Like sociable spirits everywhere, Witch City ghosts are drawn to good company . . . and there's no better place to find it than at one of Salem's great restaurants, bars, and shops.

Rockefellas

The building at Washington and Essex Streets was built for drama from the start. It began life as a theater, with world-famous actors performing live on stage. Despite the rave reviews, the high cost of the theater business was too much for the owners to bear, and the curtain closed just a few short years later.

Beginning in the 1820s, Salem's First Church held services on the second level while they rented out the first floor to shops and businesses. Through the years, these included a china shop, a bank, and a furnishings store. But the name on the front of the building today—Daniel Low & Co.—comes from the department store that occupied the building from the late 1800s to the mid-1900s. Daniel Low was a souvenir pioneer with his "witch spoon." It was one of Low's big sellers at the end of the 1800s, launching the store's mail-order business. Was

Low predicting the future success of Haunted Happenings? Maybe!)

These days, there are lots of utensils in the Daniel Low building, but they are used for eating dinner, not as souvenirs! Rockefellas restaurant is a go-to spot for steaks, seafood, and amazing burgers. The drinks menu includes lots of "mocktails" for kids, plus ice cream floats made with their "signature pop." Who could ask for more? Well, since you mentioned it. . . . The adult cocktail menu includes one mysterious mixture called "Lady in the Blue Dress." Its description reads, "After this one, you may see her." So, who is this "Lady in the Blue Dress?"

According to local lore, she was a long-ago employee of the Daniel Low & Co. department store who died at this site. No one is sure how she died, or why she might be haunting the restaurant. All they know is that in 2003, when the restaurant was just opening, an employee took a picture of the new space and she just seemed to . . . *show up*: a full-bodied apparition, right in front of the building. That's right—the owners had just poured all this time, money, effort, and heart into their restaurant, only to find out that it was haunted. What were they to do? Well, they did just what Daniel Low would have wanted them to: They sold souvenirs! T-shirts read, "Congratulations! You've Just Seen the Lady in the Blue Dress" and were given out to anyone who claimed to have had an encounter. Rockefellas posted the photo on their website. And, of course, they introduced the now-famous cocktail.

The Lady in the Blue Dress may be open to

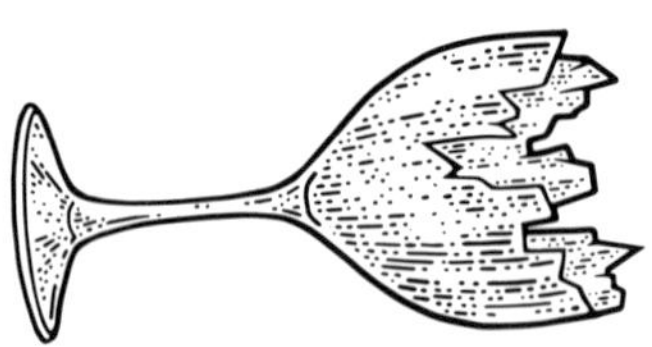

interpretation. (Was she trying to warn them away from the building or welcome them in?) However, there is another ghost at Rockefellas who is much more direct in his message. The second spirit appears to be a minister from the period when First Church met upstairs for its religious services. This fallen fellow doesn't seem to reside on the second floor, but he can be spotted in the downstairs area. Why? You can try to ask him but be warned: he's probably not going to tell you. When people have approached him, he's been known to respond, "Git, I don't want to talk to you right now." (Yikes—just asking!)

Bunghole Liquors

The very funny name of this very old shop is taken from the barrels that once held its merchandise. A "bunghole" is drilled into the side of a wine or liquor barrel to dispense the liquid within. The name is a nod to the store's beginnings, in the Prohibition era of the 1920s. During Prohibition, buying and selling alcohol was illegal in the United States, but people were still eager to buy it. So, a brisk market took off underground . . . literally, right under the current store.

In those days, the *official* business occupying this building was a funeral home. The basement level was where the staff prepared bodies for burial. The bodies were laid out on tables,

surrounded by tubes of embalming chemicals to preserve the corpses and keep them looking presentable. There was one other key feature of the basement: like other buildings near the waterfront, the building had an underground tunnel connecting directly to the wharves. In Salem's early days, tunnels like this were a sneaky way to get imported products into town without paying tariffs at the Custom House. The tunnel to the funeral home at 204 Derby Street also proved a very convenient way to roll barrels of liquor straight into the building without detection.

The funeral-home owner and his friends saw their opportunity, and soon a secret drinking club took shape in the basement: the owner, his trusted friends, and some very quiet strangers who wouldn't breathe a word of it to anyone. Meanwhile, business continued at the funeral home, with a rotating cast of characters on the embalming tables bearing silent witness to the drinking club and their subterranean shenanigans.

When Prohibition ended in 1933, Bunghole Liquors made it official: the shop was awarded Salem's second liquor license after the ban was lifted. The tables were wheeled out, embalming tubes were tucked into the walls, and the tunnel was closed up. And the many recently deceased basement bystanders who'd sat in (er, lain in?) on the basement speakeasy? Every one of the bodies was delivered to their funerals as planned. Their spirits seem to have drifted off in peace, pleased to have been invited to the party. Well, most of them, that is. One New Year's Eve, a full-bodied apparition of a woman appeared in the shop.

She walked behind a wine rack . . . then walked out again. Later in the day, she appeared again, actually bumping into a staff member—and then vanished.

More supernatural activity has been noted in the basement, where security cameras have picked up white glowing lights in the area where all those pleasant evenings passed in days gone by. Are these the joyful spirits of the drinking buddies, or spirits unknown? No one can be sure.

There's another kind of spirit here that does take a more definite form though: ghost cats. People have felt the sensation of the furry felines rubbing up against their legs . . . even when nothing is there. Ghost cats are a theme elsewhere in Salem, too. There is thought to be an abundance of ghost cats on the prowl all throughout the town. Maybe they're cruising the tunnel network—even through blocked walls. Whatever their motivation, they seem to love hanging out at this old speakeasy.

Turner's Seafood

Fish and apples? That's a taste combination that might send your stomach churning! Of course, that's not something they'd serve at Turner's Seafood. This local favorite in historic Lyceum Hall has a menu full of delicious fishy dishes and tables full of happy customers. Like everything in Salem, though, there's more to the story—including an apple orchard, a witch trial, a meeting house, a restaurant—and a spirit still churning about how it all came together!

Lyceum Hall is where Salemites once gathered to hear the great thinkers of the age talk about big ideas—literature, politics, science, and more. In this grand building in downtown Salem (rebuilt in brick after the original wooden structure burned down), poet Ralph Waldo Emerson lectured. Alexander Graham Bell demonstrated the first phone call with Salemite Thomas Watson. It was an exciting place to be. And the location couldn't be better!

Bridget Bishop had liked the location, too. After all, she had established her apple orchard in the very same spot as one of Salem's early settlers . . . before she was hauled off in 1692 to be tried and executed for witchcraft. It's said that she is not too thrilled to have a restaurant plunked right on top of her beloved orchard . . . and she shows up from time to time to let everybody know about it!

While dining at the restaurant, customers have reported spotting Bridget's image in windows and mirrors or seeing a ghostly

woman in a long white gown floating above the main staircase. Some employees have even come face-to-face with her. "When I came up the stairs and looked up, I saw another woman standing on the other staircase," said a woman who once worked in the building. The former employee described a ghostly figure in a white, seventeenth-century dress. "I was petrified. My initial thought was that a person was breaking into the restaurant. When I realized she wasn't a regular person, I ran back downstairs and almost fainted."

Meeting a ghost on the stairs does sound terrifying—especially if it is Bridget, who would have every reason to feel angry after her unjust treatment. There is also a mournfulness in the spirits here. Some people have reported seeing faces looking out the windows, hands pressed against the glass, and a general feeling of sadness. Still, it's not all negativity.

On one occasion, a ghost-hunting crew from the Travel Channel came to investigate reports of the ghostly woman's appearance in a mirror. The investigators felt sure they had found a ghost tied to the witchcraft trials, so they set up their special equipment and tried to call on her. When they did, an old cash register suddenly sprang into action and printed out a receipt. "GOOD MORNING," it read. That was strange enough . . . but the old-fashioned machine wasn't even set up to print those words!

At other times, people have smelled sweet apple blossoms in the restaurant or found fresh-picked apples where they least expect them. Maybe Bridget's message isn't meant to be scary, but helpful: a reminder of this building as a place of learning, communicating, and coming together, where our very different flavors can be *chef's kiss.*

Salem Lighthouse

Spooky Seaside

Salem has a rich seafaring past. Its ports have always been an important source of commerce, bringing much-needed imports to the colonists and, of course, a source of income. Philip English, Captain White, and others in this book made their fortunes as shipping merchants. For today's Salemites, the port is just a great place to enjoy a weekend! There's wonderful sailing, beautiful views, and a lovely selection of pirate ghosts . . . .

Derby Wharf & Customs House

This area might be your best chance to catch sight of one of Salem's seafaring ghosts!

Long ago, the Customs House—now Salem Maritime National Historic Site—was supposed to be the first stop for merchants docking in Salem. Captains would officially declare what cargo their ships were carrying, then pay fees called tariffs for the right to sell those goods. If you were a legitimate businessperson following the law, this was a regular part of doing business. If, on the other hand, you were a pirate . . . well, then you would do whatever you could to avoid paying those tariffs! That included digging underground tunnels so you could sneak things straight into your on-shore hideout . . . without ever being spotted by the Customs House.

Pirates and smugglers did dig those passageways. Today, people think the tunnels near the coast are some of the most haunted spots in town. How do they know? One sign is the high level of electromagnetic energy in the area. (Those in the know can tell they're near the tunnels when the batteries in their portable devices drain faster than usual.)

In fact, the entire area has high levels of ghost activity. You can keep an eye on your batteries for evidence, but some signs are even easier to decipher . . . especially if you stroll out over the water on the mile-long Derby Wharf.

People walking on the wharf encounter

full-body apparitions as well as cold spots on summer days. One woman reported feeling a tap on her shoulder out of the blue. When she turned around, she was face-to-face with an 1800s fisherman for just a moment . . . before he disappeared.

You might see those pirate ghosts walking out of the water near the wharf. Could they be trying to keep a low profile to sneak past the customs agents or looking for the entrance to a long-lost tunnel? We know these old privateers wouldn't want to pay if they didn't have to—maybe they are still looking for a way around the tariff, centuries after death. Other pirate captains, however, seem to seek out the Customs House: they have been witnessed there whispering to each other about the loot they've gathered on their latest adventure.

Hawthorne Cove Marina

When Mike Purcell bought his summer cottage at Hawthorne Cove Marina, he knew it was a bit of an oddball. It was reported to be a former "fish food restaurant," so he might find scales and bones between the floorboards . . . or, then again, he might find worms and goldfish flakes, used to feed fish. He knew the first level had been built in a relatively standard way, but the upstairs was actually a repurposed hull from an old boat, hoisted on top of the structure to make a second-story addition. It was a quirky old house, but it was worth learning its unusual ways to be in this amazing location: right on Salem's historic waterfront.

Still, there was something kind of spooky about the place that Mike just couldn't put his finger on. He had a feeling that he knew who could figure it out, though. Robert Ellis Cahill, the late folklorist and author of *Haunted Happenings,* was Salem's go-to guy for figuring out what exactly was haunting your house. Ghosts? Poltergeists? Residual hauntings? Or maybe just your imagination?

Mike had only felt a vague "odd energy," but when Cahill listened with his sensitive ear, he heard something very different. A "raspy, gurgling voice" growled out of nowhere, then yelled gruffly, "Get out of here!" Even the seasoned Cahill was shaken by the angry voice.

It was years before Cahill's research turned up more information about the story. At long last, he found the February 7, 1912 edition of the *Boston Daily Globe,* containing the story of the *Glendower* and its ill-fated captain Charles Wyman: "Capt. Wyman was found lying face downward in his bunk. He was dead. His face and head were covered with cuts and bruises. There were blood stains on the walls and ceiling of the cabin, although there was no sign of a struggle."

The *Glendower*'s hunchback cook, William De Graff, was charged with the crime and brought to trial. There was no convincing evidence against him, but a crew member testified hearing De Graff once say, "Captain Wyman is no good," and that the murder happened at 2:00 p.m., after De Graff's lunch shift.

Deckhand Bill Nelson took the stand and testified to hearing sounds from the captain's room at the time he died. He'd unknowingly

listened in on the victim's last words when he heard Captain Wyman shout, *"Get out of here!"*

For his defense, the humble cook had hired prestigious attorney John Feeney. It must have been an investment . . . but it paid off: De Graff was found not guilty. He walked out of the courthouse a free man and was never seen again.

Cahill later learned from a Philadelphia seaman that De Graff not only murdered Wyman, but had planned it carefully for years. The Philadelphia man, who had known both men in years past, explained what he knew: A young De Graff was climbing high in the rigging, working as a seaman on the same ship as Wyman. For some reason, Wyman was in a rage, and violently beat De Graff until he fell from the rigging onto the deck. The fall was what caused his back to become misshapen.

Wyman was the reason that De Graff could no longer climb high above the ocean, but instead was confined to the galley, feeding those who

could. So, De Graff traveled to Salem to find Wyman, joined the crew of the *Glendower*, and found his opportunity to take his revenge. But only after he'd saved enough money for the very best lawyer money could buy.

The House of the Seven Gables Museum

A Ghostly Goodbye

From scary specters to mysterious messages and whistling wanderers stuck in the mud, Salem's spirits certainly keep you on your toes! This old town's history has so much to offer: reminders to be welcoming, patient, and kind. To find inspiration everywhere. To plan your heists carefully—if you're going to steal a will, make sure it's the *real* will. And to open your senses to possibilities: take the time to listen, watch, smell, photograph, feel. That's the only way to know what your surroundings might be offering you, from this world . . . and beyond.

Enjoy your strolls through this spectacularly spooky city.

BETH HESTER is originally from the haunted city of New Orleans, where she sometimes heard ghostly footsteps in the very old house where she grew up . . . and awoke one morning to find a mysterious footprint on her ceiling! These days, she lives in New England with her husband, two children, and one spooky dog, and (most of) the footprints stay on the floor. You can find her at bethhester.com.

Check out some of the other *Spooky America* titles available now!

Spooky America was adapted from the creeptastic *Haunted America* series for adults. *Haunted America* explores historical haunts in cities and regions across America. Here's more from the original *Ghosts of Salem* author, Sam Baltrusis: